India

Tradition, Culture, and Daily Life

MAJOR NATIONS IN A GLOBAL WORLD

Books in the Series

India

Tradition, Culture, and Daily Life

MAJOR NATIONS IN A GLOBAL WORLD

Michael Centore

Mason Crest

Mason Crest
450 Parkway Drive, Suite D
Broomall, PA 19008
www.masoncrest.com

Printed and bound in the United States of America.

First printing
9 8 7 6 5 4 3 2 1

Series ISBN: 978-1-4222-3339-9
ISBN: 978-1-4222-3345-0
ebook ISBN: 978-1-4222-8585-5

The Library of Congress has cataloged the hardcopy format(s) as follows:

Library of Congress Cataloging-in-Publication Data

Centore, Michael, 1980-
  India / By Michael Centore.
      pages cm. -- (Major nations in a global world: tradition, culture, and daily life)
  Includes index.
  ISBN 978-1-4222-3345-0 (hardback) -- ISBN 978-1-4222-3339-9 (series) -- ISBN 978-1-4222-8585-5 (ebook)
  1. India--Juvenile literature. I. Title.
  DS407.C39 2015
  954--dc23
                            2015005029

Developed and produced by MTM Publishing, Inc.
        Project Director   Valerie Tomaselli
        Copyeditor   Lee Motteler/Geomap Corp.
        Editorial Coordinator   Andrea St. Aubin

Indexing Services   Andrea Baron, Shearwater Indexing

Art direction and design by Sherry Williams, Oxygen Design Group

Contents

KEY ICONS TO LOOK FOR:

Words to Understand: These words with their easy-to-understand definitions will increase the reader's understanding of the text, while building vocabulary skills.

Sidebars: This boxed material within the main text allows readers to build knowledge, gain insights, explore possibilities, and broaden their perspectives by weaving together additional information to provide realistic and holistic perspectives.

Research Projects: Readers are pointed toward areas of further inquiry connected to each chapter. Suggestions are provided for projects that encourage deeper research and analysis.

Text-Dependent Questions: These questions send the reader back to the text for more careful attention to the evidence presented there.

Series Glossary of Key Terms: This back-of-the book glossary contains terminology used throughout this series. Words found here increase the reader's ability to read and comprehend higher-level books and articles in this field.

Image of Hawa Mahal, Palace of Winds, Jaipur, India.

INTRODUCTION

A vibrant, colorful, and densely populated land, India is one of the world's most remarkable countries. Human civilization dates far back in the country, making it one of the oldest on earth. Throughout the centuries its people have survived invasions, natural disasters, and colonization to preserve their identity. Today there are over one billion residents of India, the second most after China.

Spirituality is highly valued by Indians, no matter what their faith is. The religions of Buddhism, Hinduism, Islam, and Jainism are woven into daily life. Dramatic vistas such as the towering Himalayan mountain range help convey a sense of awe and grandeur. At the same time, Indians are acutely aware of the problems facing them in the twenty-first century, especially the gap between wealthier urban areas and more impoverished rural ones. India has made great strides in becoming a global economic leader, particularly in the field of computer science, since its emancipation from British colonial power in the mid-twentieth century. It is now an exemplary democracy that respects the cultural differences of its various regions.

There is no single lens through which to understand India. Its political, spiritual, and cultural achievements have all influenced one another, shaping the history of this dynamic country.

Hindu temple of Vishnu Ranganatha Swamy in Srirangam, Tamilnadu, in east-central India.

WORDS TO UNDERSTAND

boycott: a refusal to buy a certain product as a protest against the product's maker.

infiltrate: to enter, permeate, or pass through a guarded area.

jockey: to maneuver or manipulate for an advantage; to change position by a series of movements.

nomadic: relating to people who have no fixed residence and move from place to place.

pillage: to loot, plunder, or ravage, especially in war.

CHAPTER ①

History, Religion, and Tradition

With evidence of habitation by some of the earliest human beings on the earth, India has a history as old as mankind itself. Tools dating back an incredible 2 million years have been found in the northwestern part of the country. Remnants of *Homo erectus* from between 500,000 and 200,000 years ago seem to confirm a human presence since the Stone Age. Recent discoveries of stone tools belonging to *Homo sapiens*, the descendent of *Homo erectus*, show that the first modern humans were present in India approximately 75,000 years ago.

By the time of the Bronze Age—around 3000 BCE—an extensive civilization in the valley of the Indus River of present-day Pakistan was springing to life. The Indus Valley Civilization, as it has come to be known, was one of the first urban areas in the world. Inhabitants of the Indus Valley were very advanced, constructing well-planned cities with vibrant agriculture, a system of foreign trade, and even functioning plumbing. They also developed a written language and introduced new metalworking practices, creating jewelry and other items from copper, gold, bronze, and silver.

Between 1500 and 1200 BCE, a **nomadic** group known as the Aryans migrated to the Indus Valley from the northwest. The Aryans brought with them stories about the creation of the world. Indo-Aryans began to record these stories in a written language known as Sanskrit. The resulting texts became known as the *Vedas* (meaning "wisdom"), and formed the basis of the Hindu faith. As the Aryans spread southeast, the Indus Valley Civilization gradually declined. However, by 500 BCE, another wave of urbanization occurred in the form of the sixteen *mahajanapadas*, or republics, that stretched across the north-central part of the country. This was also the time of the second major conquest of India since the Aryans, when the Persian Empire invaded from the northwest, followed by the Greeks under Alexander the Great two centuries later.

AN APTITUDE FOR MATH

Aryabhata was one of the greatest mathematicians of the Gupta Empire. He is credited with calculating the value of pi and developing a formula to find the area of a triangle.

After Alexander's army failed to **infiltrate** the depths of India, the country's first empire was established by the Mauyra dynasty, which ruled from 322 until 185 BCE. India split into a series of smaller kingdoms after the decline of the Maurya, an arrangement that lasted several hundred years. In AD 319, what became known as the "Golden Age of India" commenced with the founding of the Gupta Empire. This was a time of great cultural revival, as the fields of art, literature, architecture, philosophy, and music all flourished. Even after the Guptas lost power, the kingdoms that sprung up in their wake continued these cultural advances. They also developed new approaches to international trade and governmental administration.

Statue of Chandragupta Maurya, founder of the Maurya Empire.

THE BIRTH OF BUDDHISM

During the fifth century BCE, a man named Gautama Buddha founded one of the most serene of the world's religions, known as Buddhism. Gautama was born into a wealthy household in an area of India that is now Nepal. He abandoned his life of privilege at a young age to attain spiritual enlightenment. While meditating under a Bodhi tree one night, he received the wisdom he was seeking and began instructing others. Buddhism stresses the idea of the "Middle Way," or avoidance of extremes, as the correct approach to life.

A shrine to Buddha at the Mahabodhi Stupa, or temple, in Bodhgaya, in eastern India.

India was relatively peaceful until the dawn of the eleventh century, when once again a foreign people invaded through the northwest. This time it was the armies of the Ghaznavid Empire, led by Mahmud of Ghazni, that drove in on horses through the Khyber Pass. They did not raid the land only once, but continued to **pillage** it repeatedly—about twelve times in all—over the next thirty years. In 1175, another Muslim ruler known as Muhammad Ghori invaded in similar fashion, establishing his rule by the beginning of the thirteenth century. A series of Muslim dynasties followed, including the Khilji and the Tughlaq. In the south, the Vijayanagar Empire held power by preserving Hinduism as a unifying force amongst its people.

Elephant stables at the Sacred Center of Vijayanagara at Hampi in Karnataka, in southwestern India.

Portrait of Babur (from around 1605), leader of the Mughal Empire, which greatly increased under his rule.

In 1526, the era of divergent Muslim dynasties ended when a monarch named Babur entered India from present-day Uzbekistan to start the Mughal Empire. "Mughal" is Persian for Mongol, the group from which Babur descended. His empire quickly stretched across present-day Afghanistan, Pakistan, India, and Bangladesh. Emperors of subsequent generations—especially his grandson, Akbar—further increased the size of the empire. It was not to last, however; by the seventeenth century, the merciless sixth emperor of the dynasty, Aurangzeb, met increased resistance from both his subjects and his allies. When he died in 1707, the power of the Mughal Empire had eroded.

The palace of Fatehpur Sikri, founded by the Mughal emperor Akbar in 1569.

A LITERARY CLASSIC
Babur was a very forward thinking ruler. He enjoyed poetry and gardening, and his memoirs, the *Baburnama*, are regarded as a classic of world literature.

A painting from the *Baburnama* in the National Museum, New Delhi.

As early as the sixteenth century, the European nations of the Netherlands, France, Portugal, and Great Britain had established trading centers in India. When the Mughal Empire fell, these nations **jockeyed** for position to control European trade with India. Due to the power of Britain's navy, among other things, the British East India Company vaulted to prominence. Gradually the British government became more and more involved in the affairs of the Company. After an uprising by Hindu soldiers in 1858, the government assumed total control over the country and formally dissolved the Company. Through a highly coordinated administrative system known as the Raj, Great Britain built up infrastructure in India, though Indians were often treated as second-class citizens.

In 1915 a charismatic leader named Mohandas Gandhi began advocating for Indian independence. Through peaceful protests, **boycotts**, and other nonviolent actions, he led millions of Indians to demonstrate against British colonial rule. Finally, in 1947, the British left. To appease both the Hindu and Muslim

This colored lithograph depicts the 1858 uprising by Hindu soldiers against Britain's East India Company.

populations, India was divided into two: a vast Hindu territory and a Muslim country, known as Pakistan, divided into two regions, one in the northwest and one in the northeast of the country. (The northeastern portion would later split off into the independent country of Bangladesh in 1971.) This Partition of India, as it was called, caused great suffering, as Muslims and Hindus stranded in these newly demarcated areas were forced to flee under violent conditions to their new homes. Nevertheless, contemporary India still is home to many Muslims: Islam is practiced by some 15 percent of the population.

A COTTON MOVEMENT

In protest of British control of the textile industry, Mohandas Gandhi insisted on wearing only khadi, or cotton fabrics handwoven in India. In doing so, he led a movement to boycott British clothing made from cotton grown in India and sold back to Indians at high prices.

Mohandas Gandhi spinning his own cotton yarn in the late 1920s.

After adopting a constitution and becoming a democratic republic in 1950, India began its transition into full self-governance. It has not always been an easy road: multiple military conflicts with Pakistan, government corruption, and the assassination of Prime Minister Indira Gandhi in 1984 have all contributed to periods of unrest. While there are still tensions among the Muslim and Hindu communities, as well as socioeconomic divides reinforced by traditional class divisions known as the caste system, India today is seen as a nation on the rise. A rapidly growing economy has improved employment opportunities, particularly in the technology sector, and there are movements among citizens toward greater equality between classes.

Tourists and pilgrims visit the Raj Ghat memorial to Mohandas Gandhi located in New Delhi.

TEXT-DEPENDENT QUESTIONS

1. How did ancient Indian civilizations help advance the concept of urban living?

2. What were some of the results of the many invasions of India?

3. What events led to India becoming an independent country, and what are some of the challenges faced by contemporary Indians?

RESEARCH PROJECTS

1. Research some of the artifacts of the Indus Valley Civilization. Write a report explaining how they demonstrate advances in metalwork, sculpture, or pottery.

2. Research one of the rulers of the Mughal Empire. Write a biography outlining his life and his contributions (good or bad) to the empire.

The Gokarnanatheshwara Temple in Mangalore, Karnataka.

Women at the Surajkund Festival near Delhi.

WORDS TO UNDERSTAND

cohabitate: to live together.

modernity: the features and processes of contemporary living.

occupational: relating to one's job or vocation.

stratification: when people or things are placed in order of rank.

underpinning: something that serves as a base or support.

CHAPTER 2

Family and Friends

Friends, family, and community all play a significant role in Indian society. Families are often large, and multiple generations may live together under the same roof. Indians are a traditional people, holding fast to proven customs and routines. At times this can impinge upon social relations, as in the **stratification** of the caste system; and to some westerners, the Indian culture of prearranged marriages seems outmoded and detrimental to women's rights. Yet these traditions are ingrained in Indian life and have only recently begun to be questioned from within.

A "Hindu joint family" (or more officially a "Hindu undivided family") refers to a multigenerational Hindi family **cohabitating** in India. Generally, a Hindu

A family sits adjacent to the Golden Temple in Amritsar located in the Punjab region in northern India.

joint family consists of relatives of a common ancestor, as well as their wives, children, unmarried female siblings, and widows. When an Indian woman is married, she joins her husband's undivided family. Hindu joint families often span three generations. They live under one roof and share a single kitchen. Houses also contain a common place of worship, and family members partake of various Hindu rites and ceremonies together.

A MODEL FAMILY

Critics of the culture of individualism, waste of natural resources, and absence of community point to the Hindu joint family as a model structure of social life. In the joint family, members look after one another; they bear one another's hardships and celebrate together during times of joy; and they utilize less space and fewer natural resources than families where everyone has their own home.

Joint families are patriarchal, meaning the male head of the household (known as a *karta*) makes the major decisions involving everything from finances to the **occupational** paths of the children. The female members tend to the kitchen, cooking for the family and taking care of the youngest children. Patriarchs value the concept of seniority, meaning that the older male members have greater say in the affairs of the family than the younger. Joint families are bound by codes of cooperation, helping one another in times of crisis. The good of the family always comes before the needs of the individual members. In this regard, all property and earned income is held in common, and household expenses are shared amongst all. Property cannot be divided until the death of the *karta*.

The joint family is a structure adopted by some non-Hindus in India. For instance, some Muslim families share homes with more than one generation. For those practicing a strict form of Islam, however, the requirement to segregate women from men not their husbands makes the practice improper.

While joint families are very close knit, the caste system continues to fragment human relations in India. One of the country's oldest social institutions, it dates back to the time of the Aryan invasions of 1500 BCE. Along with various creation myths, the Aryans imported a system of social order. The four major castes, or *varnas* (a Sanskrit word meaning "colors"), each represented a particular role in society. Those of the Brahman *varna* were learned teachers and spiritual leaders. The Kshatriyas were warriors who were viewed as nobility. Traders and merchants belonged to the Vaishya *varna*, and workers were part of the Sudra *varna*. Finally, a fifth class known as the "untouchables" were seen as beneath the caste system. They performed the type of servile labor, such as making dung patties for fuel or transporting garbage, that no one else wanted to do.

In ancient India, people belonged to castes based on their skill sets and degree of intelligence rather than their status at birth. Over time, however, as castes became linked to various aspects of Hindu mythology, the concept of people being "born into" their social stations was widely accepted. Hindus believed that the different castes came from different parts of Purusha, the original cosmic man: the

Hindus in traditional clothing travel to a ceremony dedicated to Shiva at the Gangaikonda Cholapuram Temple.

Pictured here, Gandhi visits Madras, now Chennai, on a tour throughout India for the Harijan cause in 1933.

Brahmin from his mouth, the Kshatriya from his arms, the Vaishya from his legs, and the Sudra from his feet. Such theological **underpinnings** made it increasingly difficult to move between and among castes.

CHILDREN OF GOD

Gandhi advocated the use of the word "Harijan" to describe members of the untouchable class. This is translated as "child of God." Today they are sometimes referred to politically as Scheduled Castes and Scheduled Tribes. Groups such as the United Nations have introduced programs to aid their economic development.

Though firmly entrenched in Hindu culture, caste today is less a religious system and more a political one. Since the nation's independence in 1947, the Indian government has enacted rules and regulations to protect the lower castes and help facilitate social mobility. Leaders such as Mohandas Gandhi campaigned for the rights of untouchables, and the constitution of India declares the practice of untouchability to be illegal. Despite these protections, class divisions rooted in caste persist in Indian society. Untouchables (or "Dalits" in more modern terms, meaning "broken ones") are represented in business and government, yet they still face discrimination due to lingering prejudice. This is especially true in rural villages, where progressive ideas are slower to take hold.

Another tradition that has held against the pull of **modernity** is that of arranged marriages. The practice of letting one's parents or guardians select one's life partner dates back to the fourth century. Since the caste system prohibited mixing between classes and sexes, the arranged marriage was felt to be the best way to create lasting relationships. Parents could take into full consideration the social, economic, and educational background of potential mates for their sons or daughters.

When a young man reaches twenty-one and a young woman eighteen years of age, they are considered mature enough to be married. It helps if the young man has a steady source of income. The parents will let the community know when their son or daughter has expressed interest in marrying, and the process

Indian weddings, such as this one in March 2011, are colorful celebrations that continue for several days and host hundreds, sometimes thousands, of guests.

A Hindu couple during a traditional marriage ceremony.

for finding a suitable mate begins. Sometimes this involves a matchmaker, or person who specializes in pairing individuals together. With his or her help, the parents will evaluate potential matches, considering their profession, personal history, and even their horoscope. Finally, a face-to-face meeting is arranged, with the young man and his family traditionally visiting the family of the young woman. If both parties express interest, an engagement is announced.

MODERN-DAY MATCHMAKING

In the increasingly globalized, "wired" world, many Indian matchmakers have set up services online. These Internet sites post profiles of men and women seeking partners for arranged marriages. This technology has opened up the scope of arranged marriages to wider geographical areas.

There are varying opinions on arranged marriages in India. Some say it helps young people focus on finding themselves rather than worrying about finding a mate, thus making them better prepared for life partnerships. It also brings families closer together, considering the active involvement of parents in the engagement process. Finally, supporters point to the phenomenally low divorce rate in India—below 2 percent—in contrast to the 50 percent rate in America. Critics maintain that arranged marriages do not give young people sufficient choice in the matter, and that they are often based on things like social status rather than on the true character of the person involved.

TEXT-DEPENDENT QUESTIONS

1. What are the main characteristics of the Hindu joint family?
2. What are the origins of the caste system, and how has it adapted to life in India today?
3. What is the general process of an arranged marriage?

RESEARCH PROJECTS

1. Research someone from Indian history who has campaigned against the caste system, such as B. R. Ambedkar, and write a brief summary of his or her life and struggles for equality.
2. Research the tradition of the Hindu family shrine, the sacred space preserved in the home of the joint family. Write a report detailing items included in the shrine and daily family religious practices.

A Hindu ritual called "first feeding with rice" in English.

A man selling grains and beans in an open-air market.

WORDS TO UNDERSTAND

akin: alike, related, or similar.

caramelize: to change something into a caramel, a substance created by heating the sugars in foods until they become brown.

confluence: when certain elements come together.

metabolism: the bodily process of assimilating food and turning it into energy.

versatility: the ability to change or adapt to various conditions.

CHAPTER **3**

Food and Drink

The many diverse cultures that have occupied India throughout the centuries, from the Aryans over 3,000 years ago to the very recent British, have all influenced Indian cooking. This has led to a unique blend of culinary traditions. Each of India's twenty-nine states and seven union territories puts its own spin on the national cuisine, and the country's central religions—including Hinduism, Islam, and Jainism—all employ different dietary restrictions.

Despite this, there are still common ingredients used throughout the country. One such staple is the lentil. Lentils are pulses, or dried legume seeds that grow in pods. Peas and beans are other examples. Among the oldest food sources in the world, lentils are an excellent source of protein, fiber, and

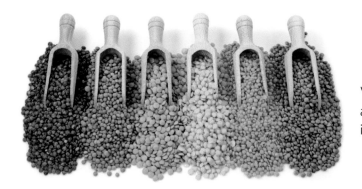

Varieties of lentils, an important staple in Indian cuisine.

Sweet pancakes called *dosa*.

Mango chutney, a popular Indian condiment.

essential amino acids. They are very inexpensive compared to other nutritional foods. In India and other places with high vegetarian populations, they are often used as a meat substitute. Their **versatility** allows them to be used in all sorts of dishes, from sweet pancakes called *dosa* for breakfast to hearty stews and soups for later in the day.

ANGLO-INDIAN CUISINE

Due to the prolonged presence of the British in India, Anglo-Indian cuisine gradually took form. This was a blend of traditional English and Indian cooking. For instance, British cooks began flavoring their standard beef stew with stronger Indian spices. They also developed their own versions of chutney, an Indian condiment similar to relish, and began incorporating it into their day-to-day fare.

One of these stews, called dal, is a classic dish in many regions of India. Technically, a dal is any type of dried pulse that has been split. There are many varieties of dal, each using a different type of pulse. What links the various dishes is the use of aromatic herbs and spices to give flavor. Most traditional dal dishes include tumeric, garlic, and onion. Fresh curry and coriander leaves as well as ginger and chili pepper are often added as well. In preparing a dal, the pulses are boiled until they have an almost porridge-like consistency. The spices and vegetables are cooked in a separate pan to preserve flavor and then added to the pulses. Depending on the pulse and spices used, the resulting dal is one of a variety of colors and textures. It is usually served with rice or an Indian bread known as roti to make a complete meal.

This dal dish, on the left, is served with rice and a type of flatbread called roti.

Chicken tikka is covered in a yogurt-and-spice marinade and cooked in a tandoor oven.

A traditional clay tandoor oven.

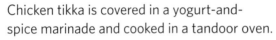

A SPECIAL OVEN

Roti and other breads are often baked in special clay ovens called tandoors, which are used throughout southern and central Asia but are said to have originated in ancient India. Tandoor ovens are used not just for bread, however, but for a wide range of food, including such well-known dishes as chicken tikka and tandoori chicken, both of which involve a yogurt-and-spice marinade.

Another ingredient that runs through the various regions of Indian cooking is a type of clarified butter called ghee. Clarified butter is made by melting butter to separate the water and milk solids from the butterfat itself; after the water evaporates and the milk solids are skimmed from the surface, only the butterfat remains. Ghee production goes one step further by **caramelizing** remnant milk solids along with the butterfat to enrich flavor.

Ghee is used in many Indian dishes, from rice to dal to sweet desserts. It is good for cooking because it does not smoke at low temperatures, as do some other oils. Additionally, it keeps much longer than regular butter. While many household cooks still make their own ghee, mass-produced versions have suffered in quality under the strain of global demand. Such "commercial" ghee is often little more than vegetable oil mixed with milk fats. Though cheaper and faster to produce, it has none of the health benefits of traditional ghee, including aiding digestion, speeding up **metabolism**, and regulating cholesterol levels.

Beyond its culinary and health properties, ghee has a special place in Indian culture as a sacred substance. Among Hindus, the cow is the most revered animal, and ghee is the most purified essence of the cow's milk. It is the only animal fat that Hindus will consume. There are references to ghee in the most ancient of

Ghee, a form of clarified butter.

Hindu scriptures, the *Rig Veda*, and other *Vedas* point to its ritualistic significance. Contemporary Hindus continue to use ghee to anoint statues of deities and as a sacrificial offering, while lamps in Hindu temples are fueled by ghee.

Indian cooking has long been affiliated with the use of spices, to the point where the nation is affectionately known as the "Spice Bowl of the World." India was a major presence in the international spice trade as far back as 3000 BCE. Thousands of years later, during the Age of Discovery, European explorers such as Vasco da Gama continued to seek India as a destination for spices. Today

India is known as the "Spice Bowl of the World" for the liberal use of spices in most of its regional cuisines.

A *lassi* seller in Varanasi.

spices remain an integral component of Indian food, especially cumin, coriander, turmeric, cardamom, and chili pepper. When used in **confluence**, these spices give Indian dishes their characteristic heat and depth of flavor.

To wash down such spicy foods, Indians enjoy a refreshing beverage called *lassi*. **Akin** in consistency to a smoothie or a milkshake, *lassi* is a blend of yogurt and water flavored with spices. Fruit, honey, salt, or other ingredients can be added to produce different variations. A popular version is the mango *lassi*, which is made with the pulp of the fruit. As these recipes become more available on a global scale, chefs from outside of India have experimented with such concoctions as an avocado-and-cucumber *lassi*. *Lassi* usually comes served in a tall glass and very cold to combat the intense Indian heat. In major Indian cities, *lassi* vendors can be seen mixing and pouring the beverage for parched passers-by.

Tea, popularized by the British, is another typical beverage in India. Indians enjoy drinking it flavored with milk, cinnamon, cloves, and other spices, a mixture called masala chai. As with *lassi*, the beverage has become internationally known, and today it is served in many coffee shops across the globe.

DESSERT INDIAN STYLE

There are many varieties of Indian desserts. Some are milk based, while others are flour based. *Kalakand* is made from a sweet milk and cheese mixture that is allowed to solidify. *Rasgulla* is also made from cheese formed into balls and soaked in a sugary syrup. *Kheer*, a rice pudding flavored with spices, raisins, and nuts, is particularly enjoyed during Hindu festivals.

Sweetened cheese balls called *rasgulla*.

TEXT-DEPENDENT QUESTIONS

1. Why is it difficult to easily summarize "Indian cuisine"?

2. For what reasons is ghee a staple in Indian cooking?

3. What have been some of the effects of globalization on Indian foods such as ghee or *lassi*?

RESEARCH PROJECTS

1. Research the cuisine particular to a region in India, such as Punjab, Rajasthan, or Tamil Nadu. Write a brief report summarizing the main ingredients used in that region, some typical dishes, and what makes its cuisine unique from the rest of the country.

2. Research a recipe for one of the many varieties of dal. With help from an adult, attempt to prepare it at home. Write a brief summary of your experience, including any difficulties you may have encountered during preparation.

Traditional snacks and foodstuffs at the Pahar Gank market in New Delhi.

A busy street in Kolkata.

WORDS TO UNDERSTAND

compulsory: mandatory; required.

curriculum: the course of study for an educational institution.

pillage: to loot, plunder, or ravage.

purveyor: one who sells or supplies an item.

sector: a subdivision of business or society.

CHAPTER 4

School, Work, and Industry

After so many years of colonial rule, India is in the midst of redefining itself as a modern power. The nation has made great advances in the field of education, including passing the Right to Education Act in 2009, which ensures "free and **compulsory**" education for children ages six through fourteen. Literacy rates have also improved dramatically over the past sixty years. Indian entrepreneurs have introduced cutting-edge industries that exist side by side with more traditional, smaller-scale artisans and craftspeople. The result of all of this is a nation trying to balance high-speed economic development with the needs of a billion citizens.

Young students learn with the help of a laptop at a rural school in West Bengal.

Modern education in India functions similarly to the European or American model, with noncompulsory preschools followed by a program of kindergarten, primary school, middle school, and secondary school. At age sixteen, there is a "higher secondary school" option for those students who may wish to continue on to university or a specialized vocational school. The university, or "graduation" level, is anywhere from three to five years, depending on subject. One to three years of "post graduation" coursework can follow. Indian schools may be public, private, or international, meaning they host students from a variety of countries.

Prior to the nineteenth century, India employed the *gurukula* system, in which students went to live with a teacher called a guru. Education was wide ranging, balancing arts and sciences with fundamental skills such as home maintenance and repair. There was often a religious component attached to the **curriculum**, as the *gurukula* system was highly revered by Hindus and Buddhists. With the rise of British colonial influence in the early nineteenth century, new educational practices were put in place that did away with the *gurukula* system. English became the official language of higher education. Rather than exchange ideas with a guru in a home-based environment, pupils now learned by rote in classrooms. While such changes introduced students to Western culture, contemporary critics point out that they may have weakened Indians' ties to their unique heritage.

A powerful symbol of India's educational history as well as its rising prominence in world affairs is the reopening of Nalanda University, which took place inSeptember 2014. The original Nalanda University was located in rural Bihar, in the northeast. It was founded in the fifth century and was among the earliest residential universities, meaning that students lived right on the grounds. At its peak it had an enrollment of 10,000—many of whom were Buddhist monks—with a faculty of 2,000. Its nine-story library was one of the best in the world. Unfortunately, the university was **pillaged** by Turkish invaders in the twelfth century, and after 800 years Nalanda was no more. In 2006 a plan was introduced to reopen the institution, and a new university was formally

The remnants of the library at Nalanda University, which is reported to have burned for three months after Turkish invaders set fire to it.

established in 2010. The full campus will be constructed on a site less than eight miles from the original location.

In addition to placing a strong emphasis on education, Indian culture also recognizes the strength of its native industries. One such example is the textile industry. India has been known as a **purveyor** of fine textiles for thousands of years; evidence suggests the practice of weaving and dyeing cotton dates back to 3000 BCE. Along with spices, textiles have been a key item of Indian trade throughout the ages, peaking in the eighteenth and nineteenth centuries. Methods such as batik (coating parts of the fabric with wax before immersing it in dye) and block printing (stamping the fabric with designs carved into wooden blocks) helped distinguish Indian textiles, and their bright colors and decorative patterns made them popular commodities in England and Europe. With the advent of the Industrial Revolution, however, machine-made textiles began to usurp handmade ones in the marketplace. Today the Indian textile industry continues to be a large part of the economy, employing over 35 million people.

Two men examine textiles, an important product of Indian manufacturers, in New Delhi.

COLORFUL DESIGNS IN FABRIC

A very complex process for adorning fabrics is known as *kalamkari*. Here, the fabric is first soaked in cow or buffalo milk and then set out to dry. Certain parts of the design are hand drawn with a bamboo pen before the fabric is soaked in a colored bath. This process is repeated for various colors, with the fabric reimmersed after every application. As with batik, wax may be used to "block off" parts of the design prior to immersion.

A less traditional but no less important portion of the Indian economy now comes from the information technology **sector**. Information technology, or IT, involves such things as telecommunications networks, computer operating systems, and Internet applications. When the United States eased immigration restrictions in the 1960s, many Indians emigrated to the country; by the 1980s, the computer revolution was underway, and there was a host of jobs to be found in programming and manufacture of personal computers. Many Indian immigrants with strong technological backgrounds filled these positions. As

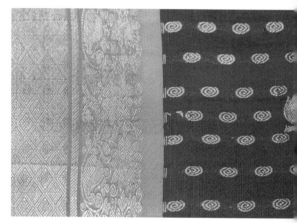

The Kancheepuram sari, a traditional dress worn by women for weddings and festivals, is made of gold *zari* and silk thread.

the industry grew, American companies looked for further opportunities to fill their technology needs abroad. India was a prime location to partner with, as a large portion of the workforce spoke English and was technologically proficient. Companies "outsourced" portions of their business to India, such as "help lines" (where customers can call for product assistance). Critics of this process say that it takes jobs from American workers, while others claim it is a benefit of globalization that injects new life into foreign economies. India's technology companies also export software and computer products to other nations, a robust business that helps make it one of the fastest-growing economies in the world.

The skyline of Bangalore, India's "Silicon Valley."

INDIA'S "SILICON VALLEY"

The city of Bangalore in the southern state of Karnataka is known as the "Silicon Valley of India." This is in reference to the "Silicon Valley" in northern California, so named for being the center of the American technology industry.

Technological advances are also on display in India's burgeoning automobile industry, and as the middle class grows, so does its desire and need for personal transportation. By some reports, India is now sixth in the world in terms of auto production, ahead of countries such as Great Britain, France, and Italy. U.S., European, and Japanese companies all have plants in India, but native Indian manufacturers, such as Tata Motors, are also responsible for India's expanding place in the global auto market.

THE TATA NANO

In 2008 Tata released the Nano as a no-frills auto: the tiny size and price tag—the equivalent of around $2,000—was meant to appeal to city dwellers needing to get around in India's increasingly congested, fast-paced cities. A second-generation Tata Nano is planned for U.S. release in 2015, with safety features upgraded—such as the inclusion of airbags—to match American regulations.

The Nano, an innovative small car made to be the least expensive in the world by the Indian auto manufacturer Tata.

TEXT-DEPENDENT QUESTIONS

1. How has the educational system in India changed throughout time?

2. How does the reopening of Nalanda University link the present with the past?

3. What factors caused the growth of the information technology sector in India?

RESEARCH PROJECTS

1. Research a school, university, madrassa, or other educational institution in India. Write a brief report detailing its history, curriculum, and approach to education. How does it differ from its American counterpart? How is it similar?

2. Research another small-scale industry in India, such as wood or stone carving or carpet weaving. Write a brief report about the current state of the industry, its main centers of practice, and the challenges it might face due to large-scale industrialization.

A rickshaw drives through a crowded street in Lucknow, in northern India.

Dancers performing at the Hindu Holi Festival.

WORDS TO UNDERSTAND

facet: one aspect of a larger subject.

facilitate: to make something possible.

improvisation: the act of creating or composing something in the moment.

liturgical: relating to liturgy, or the customs of worship for a particular religion.

monsoon: a very heavy rainfall associated with the weather patterns of southern Asia.

CHAPTER 5

Arts and Entertainment

Considering its long and varied history, it is no wonder that India has been able to establish fertile musical, literary, and artistic traditions. The *Vedas*, the oldest of the Hindu scriptures, had great influence on the formation of the arts in India. With the arrival of different foreign cultures over the years, including the Persian Mughuls and the British, Indian arts were exposed to a wide variety of new theories and practices. This combination of deep tradition and cultural blending has given India a unique place within art history and has helped **facilitate** the production of many lasting works.

While the arts occupy a great place in daily life, Indians value any form of entertainment that helps bring people together. One such example is Makar Sankranti. This holiday commemorates the day when the sun enters the sign of

Hundreds of people gather on the banks of the Ganges River in Haridwar, in northern India, to celebrate Makar Sankranti, a festival honoring the beginning of the harvest.

Capricorn and begins its passage from the Southern to the Northern Hemisphere. Daylight starts to increase around this time, and so the festival is seen as a celebration of new beginnings, primarily that of the harvest season. It is also the time when the season of **monsoons** finally tapers off in southern India.

Makar Sankranti has Hindu origins but is celebrated all over India and Nepal. Different regions of India call the holiday by different names and have different customs. For example, in Punjab the festival is known as Lorhi, and large bonfires are lit just before sunset in town squares. Residents gather around to toss candy, sesame seeds, and *gur*—a product made from boiling sugarcane juice—into the fire as offerings. In Gujarat, special emphasis is placed on the relationship between the old and the young. Gifts are exchanged between relatives, and people of all ages fly colorful kites. Those in the state of Tamil Nadu refer to the holiday as "Pongal." It is spread out over four days. On the first day, celebrants clean out their wardrobes for the coming spring. They make a dish of rice, boiled milk, nuts, and raisins on the second day, using it as an offering to an ancestral god. The third day is devoted to expressing gratitude for cattle, while the fourth is spent relaxing among family and friends.

THE END OF A SEASON

Another important Hindu festival celebrated all over India is Diwali. As Makar Sankranti foretells the forthcoming harvest season, Diwali marks the end of a harvest cycle. It is a five-day event celebrated in late October or early November. Hindus refer to it as the "festival of lights," as they set out clay lamps and candles around their homes to symbolize inner light overcoming the world's darkness.

As with most Indian holidays, music plays a large part in creating a festive atmosphere during Makar Sankranti. Beyond holidays, however, music is a main component of Indian cultural identity. The origins of Indian classical music are believed to date back 3,000 years to the Indus Valley Civilization, though it was not until musicians began composing chants for the Vedic hymns that a workable tradition emerged. These rhythmic chants eventually developed into ragas, or the "scales" of Indian music.

Traditional Indian musicians from the north of the country play local instruments in Delhi.

Ragas may be associated with particular seasons or times of the day, and they are often used as aids to meditation. There are approximately 150 ragas in use today. Each raga utilizes different patterns of notes to create a melody. Atmosphere and feeling are more important in the playing of a raga than the notes themselves. Ragas are unique in that they are not written by single composers but rather brought to life by the players: musicians follow rules of **improvisation** to "color" the raga according to their inner emotional state.

KEEPING TIME WITH TALAS

Percussionists must follow specific patterns called talas. In the way a raga determines a melody, a tala determines the rhythm. It comes from the Hindi word *tali*, meaning "clap." Talas work in cycles, meaning they begin with a specific beat, are developed, and come back to the original beat at various points throughout the raga.

The instruments used to create Indian classical music are quite varied. Perhaps the most well known is the sitar, a stringed instrument that can be tuned in many ways to accommodate different ragas. There are up to twenty strings on a sitar. The tabla is a percussive instrument used to keep rhythm. It is made of two hand drums, one slightly larger than the other. The player uses deft movements of palms and fingers to create different pitches as he or she manip-

Prominent sitar player, Ustad Shammin Ahmed Khan (center), performs with fellow musicians at a premier school in Mumbai (Bombay).

A Lady Playing the Tanpura by Kishangarh Rajasthan (1735). The tanpura, or tambura, is a stringed instrument similar to the sitar.

ulates the drums. A third key Indian instrument is the tambura. Like the sitar, this is a stringed instrument with a long neck and hollow body. Rather than providing a melody, the role of the tambura is to accompany the other instruments with a drone, or a singular note that resonates throughout the piece. The tambura has four strings and no frets, and the player must be deft in his or her timing to sustain the drone.

TWO STRAINS OF INDIAN CLASSICAL MUSIC

There are two main types of Indian classical music: Hindustani, played mostly in the north, and Carnatic in the south. They each use slightly different melodic and rhythmic systems and have different names for certain ragas. Hindustani music places greater emphasis on improvisation, while Carnatic is more tied to compositional structures.

The base text of Indian literature—and for many of the Indian arts in general—is the *Vedas*. As the oldest of the Hindu scriptures, they are primarily religious in nature; however, since they speak on diverse **facets** of the human condition, their influence has seeped into many areas of Indian life. It is difficult to pinpoint the exact date of their composition, as they were kept alive by oral tradition for hundreds of years before being compiled and written down. A common Hindu belief is that the *Vedas* have existed since time immemorial and were passed directly from God to man. One scholarly theory holds that they were brought to India by migrant Aryans around 1500 BCE, but were not recorded until sometime after 300 BCE. When they were finally written, it was in a language called Sanskrit, among the oldest in the world.

The *Vedas* are divided into four sections: the *Rig Veda*, the *Sama Veda*, the *Yajur Veda*, and the *Atharva Veda*. The *Rig Veda* is the largest of the *Vedas*, divided into ten books called mandalas. It contains 1,028 hymns for recitation. The *Sama Veda* is essentially an assemblage of melodies to be used with the words of the *Rig Veda*. The *Yajur Veda* contains the words for ancient

An early nineteenth-century manuscript of the *Rig Veda*, the longest of the *Vedas*.

Hindu **liturgical** acts, while the *Atharva Veda* is a collection of hymns, spells, and prayers written in a more down-to-earth style than those of the other *Vedas*. The rich spiritual language of the *Vedas* continues to echo throughout contemporary Hindu society, shaping thought, artistic and legal customs, and ritual observances.

DRAWING NEAR TO THE *VEDAS*

The *Upanishads* are texts related to the *Vedas* that were composed between 800 and 200 BCE. The word *Upanishad* means "sitting close to," a reference to a student approaching a spiritual teacher. In this fashion, the *Upanishads* "draw near to" the *Vedas* by commenting upon them, elaborating on their teachings and their stories of the world's creation.

One of India's most popular preoccupations—cricket—is as secular as the *Vedas* are spiritual. The British East India Company brought the game—played with bat and ball by eleven players dressed in white in a large field

with a rectangular "pitch" at its center—to India, but the pastime far outlasted British rule. India consistently performs well in international cricket competitions, and its fan base is massive, supporting the largest cricket stadium in the world in Kolkata (Calcutta), East Gardens, which holds over 90,000 people.

A cricket match played at Pune, in western India, between India and Australia.

TEXT-DEPENDENT QUESTIONS

1. How do Makar Sankranti celebrations differ in various parts of India?
2. What are some key components (e.g., melodic structures or instruments) of Indian classical music?
3. Why have the *Vedas* had such a pervasive influence on Indian culture?

RESEARCH PROJECTS

1. Research another holiday celebrated in India, perhaps by Buddhists (e.g., Buddha Purnima) or Jains (e.g., Mahavir Jayanti). Write a brief report summarizing its history, what it commemorates, and how it is celebrated.
2. Research an Indian artist of a discipline of your choosing, such as a poet, painter, or musician. Write a brief biography of his or her life, including how Indian culture shaped his or her work.

A woman painting in the Madhubani style.

A tea plantation in Munnar, Kerala, in southwestern India.

WORDS TO UNDERSTAND

complex: hard to separate, analyze, or solve.

laypeople: members of a religion who are not priests, monks, or other clergy.

manifest: to make evident by showing or presenting.

mausoleum: a large building that contains a tomb or burial chamber.

renounce: to give something up.

CHAPTER 6

Cities, Towns, and the Countryside

The physical topography and social landscape of India is one of great extremes. From the towering peaks of the Himalayas in the northeast and the vast, arid stretch of the Great Indian Desert in the northwest to the tropical regions of the south, the country is home to an astounding array of terrain and climate systems. Its billion residents are divided between isolated, often impoverished rural areas and densely populated megalopolises such as Mumbai (Bombay) and Delhi. As the economy grows at a rapid rate, the gap between the rich and poor continues to widen, making more **complex** the social fabric of this already complicated place.

The Taj Mahal, one of the most recognized structures in the world, was a massive endeavor that took over twenty years to complete.

In the midst this changing environment, certain landmarks lend a sense of stability. Undoubtedly, one of the most recognizable is the Taj Mahal. Located in Agra, Uttar Pradesh, in the north-central part of India, the Taj Mahal was built between 1632 and 1653 by the Mughal emperor Shah Jahan. He intended it as a memorial to his deceased wife, Mumtaz Mahal, and spared no expense to ensure its exquisite design. It is believed that over 20,000 workers were involved in its construction. While the Taj Mahal is today seen as a masterpiece of Muslim architecture, it is curious that the name of its head architect has been lost to history. Scholars now know the building was designed by committee, with Shah Jahan taking an active role in shaping the plans.

The Taj Mahal is not just one building, but an entire complex that includes a **mausoleum**, a mosque, extensive gardens, massive gateways, a guesthouse, and additional tombs. The mausoleum is perhaps the most striking component: it is built entirely of marble and is capped with a dome 115 feet in height; its site is framed by four minarets that rise 130 feet into the sky. In addition, there are intricate carvings on both the exterior and interior walls, as well as designs created with inlaid stone. Some of the carvings reproduce passages from the *Koran*, the sacred book of Islam. The gardens are equally eye-catching, laid out in a symmetrical pattern with numerous fountains, a reflecting pool, and rows of neatly planted cypress trees. Even the auxiliary buildings, such as the red sandstone guesthouse, were built with exquisite attention to detail and proportional symmetry.

BUILDING THE TAJ MAHAL

In addition to the 20,000 workers, it is estimated that a thousand elephants were used in the building of the Taj Mahal. They hauled materials that were otherwise too heavy or unwieldy to carry. A beautiful feature of the white marble building is the way it reflects the varying sunlight throughout the day. If there is a full moon, the surface turns a soft golden color.

Calligraphy, or ornamental text, is inscribed on many of the structures of the Taj Mahal.

Many shades of blue give Jodhpur its nickname, "The Blue City."

The architectural integrity of the Taj Mahal is **manifested** in a different way in the city of Jodhpur. With over a million residents, it is the second largest city in the state of Rajasthan in the northwestern part of the country. Its main landmark is the Mehrangarh Fort, a massive military outpost built in the fifteenth century and located high above the city. However, it is what lies below the fort that gives Jodhpur its nickname of the "Blue City": a dense collection of dwellings spread over the hillside, each one painted a shade of blue. The expanse of unified color is a unique and beautiful sight, particularly as the houses are set against the backdrop of the arid Thar Desert. One theory as to why residents continue to paint their houses blue is that the color wards off the heat—Jodhpur is known as "Sun City," an apt description of its weather. Another is that residents are simply adopting a tradition begun when Jodhpur's Brahmins (the highest group in the Indian caste system) painted their homes to distinguish themselves.

DEFENDING JODHPUR

In addition to the Mehrangarh Fort, a wall surrounds Jodhpur as a relic from its more defense-minded past. Today the limits of the city have expanded well outside the wall, but within is still the "old city": open markets, narrow streets, and artisans preserving the techniques of their ancestors.

A common site in the cities, towns, and countryside of India are wandering sadhus, or holy men and women of the Hindu faith. Sadhu means "good man" in Sanskrit; the feminine form is *sadhvi*. Sadhus **renounce** all ties to their friends, family, and material possessions in order to seek enlightenment, or union with the divine. Sadhus also forsake the notion of caste. Some sadhus live collectively in monastic communities, while others occupy caves, hermitages, or other solitary places. Most are itinerant, meaning they move from place to place, routing through the many sacred sites of Hinduism. On this pilgrimage they carry few possessions: a begging bowl, prayer beads, and perhaps a walking staff and teapot. Non-sadhus whom they encounter on their way offer them food, hoping to obtain their blessing.

THE MARKINGS OF A SADHU

Sadhus usually wear orange or yellow robes, though some wear only a simple loincloth. They may grow their hair and beards and let them become matted over time. Some adorn their bodies with painted designs, or cover them in ash as a reminder of their mortality. Others apply a simple mark on their forehead called a *tilaka*; depending on the color or material used, the *tilaka* has special significance.

Every third year, there is a massive gathering of sadhus and millions of Hindu **laypeople** known as Kumbh Mela. It occurs on a rotating basis on the shores of rivers in one of four locations: Haridwar (on the Ganges), Nasik, Ujjain, and Allahabad. The central event is a ritual bath. Before dawn, millions

of attendees begin plunging into the river in hopes of purifying their souls and the souls of their ancestors. The day continues as pilgrims visit one another, discuss religious concepts, meet with sadhus to receive words of wisdom, pray and chant, and share simple meals. Kumbh Mela is the largest religious assembly in the world.

A sadhu man sits near the water in Varanasi, in northern India.

Nashik, one of the rotating sites of Kumbh Mela, is a metropolitan center of around 1.5 million people. One of India's oldest but fastest-growing urban areas, it is the home of over 100 ancient temples as well as a growing aeronautics industry, a pharmaceutical center, and business outsourcing companies. This blend of the historical and the modern is a marker of India's major urban centers. For instance, New Delhi, the capital, which counts around 22 million as its residents and is the country's largest city in terms of population, has a built environment reflecting its storied past—including palaces and fortresses of Mughal rulers, such as the famous Red Fort in the Shahjahanabad district, alongside monuments to the British Empire.

Stalls selling fireworks in Nashik, one of the rotating sites for the Kumbh Mela festival.

TEXT-DEPENDENT QUESTIONS

1. What are the components of the Taj Mahal, and why are they so unique?

2. Why do you think Jodhpur continually ranks as one of the most popular tourist destinations in India?

3. What characteristics differentiate sadhus from the rest of the Indian population?

RESEARCH PROJECTS

1. Research a historical monument in India, such as the Hawa Mahal or the Sanchi Stupa. Write a brief report detailing its history, how it was constructed, and its past as well as present significance.

2. Research one of the six major climate zones spread across India. Write a brief report detailing how the climate impacts cities and/or the countryside, and the advantages and disadvantages it provides Indian residents.

The Moosi Maharani Chhatri memorial in Alwar, in northwestern India.

FURTHER RESEARCH

Online

View statistics, maps, and a brief history about India on the Central Intelligence Agency's World Factbook: https://www.cia.gov/library/publications/the-world-factbook/geos/in.html.

There are hundreds of things to learn about India on its official government website: http://india.gov.in.

Learn more about tourism in India by visiting http://www.incredibleindia.org/en/ as well as India's official Ministry of Tourism website, http://tourism.gov.in.

Check out one woman's blog about her journey with Indian food and with life: http://www.indianfoodrocks.com.

Books

Eck, Diana L. *India: A Sacred Geography*. New York: Harmony Books, 2013.

Guha, Ramachandra. *India After Gandhi: The History of the World's Largest Democracy*. New York: Harper Perennial, 2008.

Keay, John. *India: A History*. New York: Grove Press, 2011.

Luce, Edward. *In Spite of the Gods: The Rise of Modern India*. New York: Anchor Books, 2008.

NOTE TO EDUCATORS: This book contains both imperial and metric measurements as well as references to global practices and trends in an effort to encourage the student to gain a worldly perspective. We, as publishers, feel it's our role to give young adults the tools they need to thrive in a global society.

SERIES GLOSSARY

ancestral: relating to ancestors, or relatives who have lived in the past.

archaeologist: a scientist that investigates past societies by digging in the earth to examine their remains.

artisanal: describing something produced on a small scale, usually handmade by skilled craftspeople.

colony: a settlement in another country or place that is controlled by a "home" country.

commonwealth: an association of sovereign nations unified by common cultural, political, and economic interests and traits.

communism: a social and economic philosophy characterized by a classless society and the absence of private property.

continent: any of the seven large land masses that constitute most of the dry land on the surface of the earth.

cosmopolitan: worldly; showing the influence of many cultures.

culinary: relating to the kitchen, cookery, and style of eating.

cultivated: planted and harvested for food, as opposed to the growth of plants in the wild.

currency: a system of money.

demographics: the study of population trends.

denomination: a religious grouping within a faith that has its own organization.

dynasty: a ruling family that extends across generations, usually in an autocratic form of government, such as a monarchy.

ecosystems: environments where interdependent organisms live.

endemic: native, or not introduced, to a particular region, and not naturally found in other areas.

exile: absence from one's country or home, usually enforced by a government for political or religious reasons.

feudal: a system of economic, political, or social organization in which poor landholders are subservient to wealthy landlords; used mostly in relation to the Middle Ages.

globalization: the processes relating to increasing international exchange that have resulted in faster, easier connections across the world.

gross national product: the measure of all the products and services a country produces in a year.

heritage: tradition and history.

homogenization: the process of blending elements together, sometimes resulting in a less interesting mixture.

iconic: relating to something that has become an emblem or symbol.

idiom: the language particular to a community or class; usually refers to regular, "everyday" speech.

immigrants: people who move to and settle in a new country.

indigenous: originating in and naturally from a particular region or country.

industrialization: the process by which a country changes from a farming society to one that is based on industry and manufacturing.

SERIES GLOSSARY

integration: the process of opening up a place, community, or organization to all types of people.

kinship: web of social relationships that have a common origin derived from ancestors and family.

literacy rate: the percentage of people who can read and write.

matriarchal: of or relating to female leadership within a particular group or system.

migrant: a person who moves from one place to another, usually for reasons of employment or economic improvement.

militarized: warlike or military in character and thought.

missionary: one who goes on a journey to spread a religion.

monopoly: a situation where one company or state controls the market for an industry or product.

natural resources: naturally occurring materials, such as oil, coal, and gold, that can be used by people.

nomadic: describing a way of life in which people move, usually seasonally, from place to place in search of food, water, and pastureland.

nomadic: relating to people who have no fixed residence and move from place to place.

parliament: a body of government responsible for enacting laws.

patriarchal: of or relating to male leadership within a particular group or system.

patrilineal: relating to the relationship based on the father or the descendants through the male line.

polygamy: the practice of having more than one spouse.

provincial: belonging to a province or region outside of the main cities of a country.

racism: prejudice or animosity against people belonging to other races.

ritualize: to mark or perform with specific behaviors or observances.

sector: part or aspect of something, especially of a country's or region's economy.

secular: relating to worldly concerns; not religious.

societal: relating to the order, structure, or functioning of society or community.

socioeconomic: relating to social and economic factors, such as education and income, often used when discussing how classes, or levels of society, are formed.

statecraft: the ideas about and methods of running a government.

traditional: relating to something that is based on old historical ways of doing things.

urban sprawl: the uncontrolled expansion of urban areas away from the center of the city into remote, outlying areas.

urbanization: the increasing movement of people from rural areas to cities, usually in search of economic improvement, and the conditions resulting this migration.

INDEX

Italicized page numbers refer to illustrations.

INDEX

INDEX

INDEX

PHOTO CREDITS

ABOUT THE AUTHOR

Michael Centore is a writer and editor. He has helped produce many titles, including memoirs, cookbooks, and educational materials, among others, for a variety of publishers. He has experience in several facets of book production, from photo research to fact checking. His poetry and essays have appeared in *Crux*, *Tight*, *Mockingbird*, and other print- and web-based publications. Prior to his involvement in publishing, he worked as a stone mason, art handler, and housepainter. He was born in Hartford, Connecticut, and lives in Brooklyn, New York.